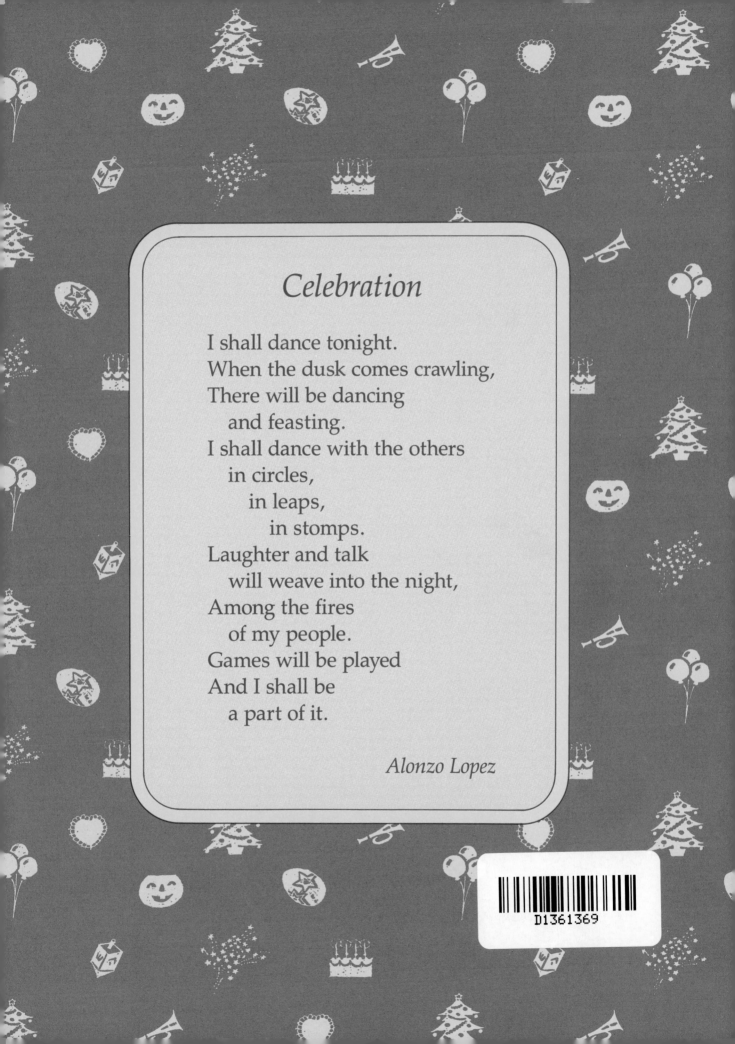

Celebration

I shall dance tonight.
When the dusk comes crawling,
There will be dancing
    and feasting.
I shall dance with the others
    in circles,
        in leaps,
            in stomps.
Laughter and talk
    will weave into the night,
Among the fires
    of my people.
Games will be played
And I shall be
    a part of it.

Alonzo Lopez

Little People™ Big Book

About
HOLIDAYS
and
CELEBRATIONS

TIME
LIFE *for*
Children™

ALEXANDRIA, VIRGINIA

Table of Contents

New Year's Day

Last night, while we were fast asleep,
The old year went away.
It can't come back again because
A new one's come to stay.

Rachel Field

4

CELEBRATING NEW YEAR'S AROUND THE WORLD

Most of us celebrate New Year's on January 1, which is a very special day. On this day, we wish each other well for the twelve months to come by saying, "HAPPY NEW YEAR!"

In some countries, people begin their new year on different days. Each country has its own festive customs and traditional ways of celebrating the New Year's holiday. Which way sounds best to you?

Bong! Bong! Bong! All across Denmark, clocks are chiming. It's midnight on December 31—New Year's Eve. Erik, Britta, Mommy, and Daddy run into the streets, shouting, "Godt Nytar" (god nu-*taar*) as loud as they can. They welcome the New Year by banging on pots and pans—it's the noisiest night of the year!

Squeak! Squeak! Jacques and Nicole are using markers to write out their New Year's wishes on colored paper. In Belgium, this is what all the children do. Jacques wishes the new baby will be a boy. Nicole wishes that her friend, Isabel, will come to visit. On New Year's Day, the children read their wishes to their parents. When they finish, they wish each other a Happy New Year by saying "Bonne Année" (bon an-*ee*).

Ding Dong! In North Carolina, Grandpa opens the door. "Happy New Year!" shout Kathy and Michael, who have come to visit. There's no school or work on January 1, New Year's Day, so everyone gets to be together. Grandma is in the kitchen making hoppin' John—a yummy dish of black-eyed peas and rice. Families all across the southern United States eat it too, so they can have good luck all year long!

Crack! Pop! Pow! Liang and Mu Lan cover their ears as firecrackers burst through the dark night. It's the Chinese New Year's parade, which takes place in January or March. Their favorite float is the silk and bamboo dragon that winds down the street scaring away evil spirits. "Xin nien quai ler!" (*seen yen qwai la*) shouts everybody. That means "Happy New Year."

Swish! Swish! In India, Valli and her sisters walk around in their silky new saris. They are dressed up to celebrate the Hindu New Year, which comes each year during April or May. Today, Grandfather takes Valli's brother, Rama, into the waters of the Ganges River. "It'll bring us good luck all year long," says Grandfather.

Tequi'ah! Amit loves the deep rich sound of the *shofar*, or ram's horn, as it fills the synagogue. In Israel, and around the world, Jews celebrate Rosh Hashanah, the Jewish New Year, in September or October. Everybody says "Shanah tovah" (shah-*nah* toe-*vah*) to each other, which means "Happy New Year." Amit knows it's a time to think about how he behaved last year. But he can't help also thinking about his favorite holiday food—apples and honey for a sweet New Year!

New Year's Hats for the Statues

*A Japanese Tale by Yoshiko Uchida,
adapted from Kasa Jizo*

nce a very kind old man and woman lived in a small house high in the hills of Japan. Although they were good people, they were very, very poor, for the old man made his living by weaving the reed hats that farmers used to ward off the sun and rain, and even in a year's time, he could not sell very many.

One cold winter day as the year was drawing to an end, the old woman said to the old man, "Good husband, it will soon be New Year's Day, but we have nothing in the house to eat. How will we welcome the new year without even a pot of fresh rice?" A worried frown hovered over her face, and she sighed sadly as she looked into her empty cupboards.

But the old man patted her shoulders and said, "Now, now, don't you worry. I will make some reed hats and take them to the village to sell. Then with the money I earn I will buy some fish and rice for our New Year's feast."

10

On the day before New Year's, the old man set out for the village with five new reed hats that he had made. It was bitterly cold, and from early morning, snow tumbled from the skies and blew in great drifts about their small house. The old man shivered in the wind, but he thought about the fresh warm rice and the fish turning crisp and brown over the charcoal, and he knew he must earn some money to buy them. He pulled his wool scarf tighter about his throat and plodded on slowly over the snow-covered roads.

When he got to the village, he trudged up and down its narrow streets calling, "Reed hats for sale! Reed hats for sale!" But everyone was too busy preparing for the New Year to be bothered with reed hats. They scurried by him, going instead to the shops where they could buy sea bream and red beans and herring roe for their New Year's feasts. No one even bothered to look at the old man or his hats.

As the old man wandered about the village, the snow fell faster, and before long the sky began to grow dark. The old man knew it was useless to linger, and he sighed with longing as he passed the fish shop and saw the rows of fresh fish.

"If only I could bring home one small piece of fish for my wife," he thought glumly, but his pockets were even emptier than his stomach.

There was nothing to do but to go home again with his five unsold hats. The old man headed wearily back toward his little house in the hills, bending his head against the biting cold of the wind. As he walked along, he came upon six stone statues of Jizo, the guardian god of children. They stood by the roadside covered with snow that had piled in small drifts on top of their heads and shoulders.

"*Mah, mah*, you are covered with snow," the old man said to the statues, and setting down his bundle, he stopped to brush the snow from their heads. As he was about to go on, a fine idea occurred to him.

"I am sorry these are only reed hats I could not sell," he apologized, "but at least they will keep the snow off your heads." And carefully he tied one on each of the Jizo statues.

"Now if I had one more there would be enough for each of them," he murmured as he looked at the row of statues. But the old man did not hesitate for long. Quickly he took the hat from his own head and tied it on the head of the sixth statue.

"There," he said looking pleased. "Now all of you are covered." Then, bowing in farewell, he told the statues that he must be going. "A Happy New Year to each of you," he called, and he hurried away content.

When he got home the old woman was waiting anxiously for him. "Did you sell your hats?" she asked. "Were you able to buy some rice and fish?"

The old man shook his head. "I couldn't sell a single hat," he explained, "but I did find a very good use for them." And he told her how he had put them on the Jizo statues that stood in the snow.

"Ah, that was a very kind thing to do," the old woman said. "I would have done exactly the same." And she did not complain at all that the old man had not brought home anything to eat. Instead she made some hot tea and added a precious piece of charcoal to the brazier so the old man could warm himself.

That night they went to bed early, for there was no more charcoal and the house had grown cold. Outside the wind continued to blow the snow in a white curtain that wrapped itself about the small house. The old man and woman huddled beneath their thick quilts and tried to keep warm.

13

"We are fortunate to have a roof over our heads on such a night," the old man said.

"Indeed we are," the old woman agreed, and before long they were both fast asleep.

About daybreak, when the sky was still a misty gray, the old man awakened, for he heard voices outside.

"Listen," he whispered to the old woman.

"What is it? What is it?" the old woman asked.

Together they held their breath and listened. It sounded like a group of men pulling a very heavy load.

"*Yoi-sah! Hoi-sah! Yoi-sah! Hoi-sah!*" the voices called and seemed to come closer and closer.

"Who could it be so early in the morning?" the old man wondered. Soon, they heard the men singing.

"Where is the home of the kind old man,
 The man who covered our heads?
 Where is the home of the kind old man,
 Who gave us his hats for our heads?"

The old man and woman hurried to the window to look out, and there in the snow they saw the six stone Jizo statues lumbering toward their house. They still wore the reed hats the old man had given them, and each one was pulling a heavy sack.

"*Yoi-sah! Hoi-sah! Yoi-sah! Hoi-sah!*" they called as they drew nearer and nearer.

"They seem to be coming here!" the old man gasped in amazement. But the old woman was too surprised even to speak.

As they watched, each of the Jizo statues came up to their house and left his sack at the doorstep.

The old man hurried to open the door, and as he did, the six big sacks came tumbling inside. In the sacks the old man and woman found rice and wheat, fish and beans, wine and bean paste cakes, and all sorts of delicious things that they might want to eat.

"Why, there is enough here for a feast every day all during the year!" the old man cried excitedly.

"And we shall have the finest New Year's feast we have ever had in our lives," the old woman exclaimed.

"Ojizo Sama, thank you!" the old man shouted.

"Ojizo Sama, how can we thank you enough?" the old woman called out.

But the six stone statues were already moving slowly down the road, and as the old man and woman watched, they disappeared into the whiteness of the falling snow, leaving only their footprints to show that they had been there at all.

To My Valentine

If apples were pears,
And peaches were plums,
And the rose had a different name;
If tigers were bears,
And fingers were thumbs,
I'd love you just the same!

Unknown

There are lots of colorful Valentine hearts in this classroom.
Can you find ten red hearts?
Can you find eight purple hearts?
Now try to find four yellow hearts and three blue hearts.
Which color is your favorite?

The First Easter Rabbit

A Retelling of a Traditional Tale

There was once a time, many years ago, when winter came and stayed longer than ever. In fact, it stayed so long that the children grew tired of playing in the snow, of sledding on the hill, and of building snowmen in the fronts of houses. Spring was their favorite time of year, and when it didn't come, the children ran to the woods to look for it. They searched the nooks and hollows for baby rabbits, and the trees for squirrels and chipmunks and birds. They searched high and low for their woodland friends who returned every spring, but alas, they were nowhere to be found. What if spring never comes? they wondered miserably, as they headed to their homes through the graying snow.

18

But that night, as the children were sleeping, the world outdoors started to change. The rabbits and the squirrels and the other woodland creatures came out of their winter hiding places and looked around. Even the robin redbreasts appeared.

"Where are the children?" the animals wondered. "The children are always here to greet us. We are lonely without the children."

"Perhaps they don't think spring is coming this year," the robin suggested.

"After all," added the fox, "we were all mighty late."

"Then someone must go and tell them that we're here," said the squirrel. "Robin Redbreast, you fly to town and let the children know that we've come."

"I wish I could," said the robin, "but I must finish building my nest. Why don't you go, Fox?"

"I'd be happy to, but the townsfolk would run me off. Black Bear, can you go?"

"I'm sorry to say," growled the bear, "that the children are a little afraid of me."

This was true. Then they all turned to look at the rabbit.

"Rabbit," said the robin, "you have always been the children's favorite. Why don't you go?"

The rabbit shrank back. "Oh, no! I am far too shy."

"Then go at night," the others suggested.

"But the children are asleep at night," said Rabbit. "How will they know that I've come?"

The animals all put their heads together and formed a plan. And a splendid plan it was!

First, the birds gathered twigs and vines, and with their clever beaks, they wove a basket. Meanwhile, the bears were busily pulling up sweet tender shoots of grass to line the basket. Next, the squirrels came scampering to fill the basket with nuts. Last, but by no means least, each bird brought an egg from her nest to lay in the basket. Each egg was different—the robin's egg, as blue as the sky; the sparrow's egg, speckled brown; the oriole's, as brown as richest milk chocolate. Over the eggs, the animals sprinkled flowers.

That night, the rabbit took the basket and hopped off to town. As the children slept, the rabbit stopped at each doorstep and left a small nest of grass containing some nuts, an egg or two, and a sprinkling of flowers.

The next morning dawned fair and bright. The children ran outside. Imagine their delight upon finding the presents on their doorsteps! And there was no mistaking whose footprints were in the soft spring earth.

"Hooray!" they shouted and kicked up their heels. "Winter has gone away and spring has come! The rabbit came last night to tell us!" Then off they ran to the woods to greet their woodland pals.

Ever since that time, the rabbit has come every year, carrying a basket brimming with goodies. He leaves a little something for every boy and girl as a sign that spring has come. And now you know how the Easter Rabbit came to be.

EASTER EGG HUNT

The Easter Rabbit, Robin Redbreast, Fox, and Black Bear are searching for Easter eggs. And they need your help! There are twenty eggs hidden in the picture. Can you find them all?

Little Black Hen

Berryman and Baxter,
 Prettiboy and Penn
And old Farmer Middleton
 Are five big men . . .
And all of them were after
 The Little Black Hen.

She ran quickly,
 They ran fast;
Baxter was first, and
 Berryman was last.

I sat and watched
   By the old plum-tree . . .
She squawked through the hedge
   And she came to me.

The Little Black Hen
   Said, "Oh, it's you!"
I said, "Thank you,
   How do you do?
And please will you tell me,
   Little Black Hen,
What did they want,
   Those five big men?"

The Little Black Hen
   She said to me:
"They want me to lay them
   An egg for tea.
If they were Emperors,
   If they were Kings,
I'm much too busy
   To lay them things."

"I'm not a King
   And I haven't a crown;
I climb up trees,
   And I tumble down.
I can shut one eye,
   I can count to ten,
So lay me an egg, please,
   Little Black Hen."

The Little Black Hen said,
   "What will you pay,
If I lay you an egg
   For Easter Day?"

25

"I'll give you a Please
    And a How-do-you-do,
I'll show you the Bear
    Who lives in the Zoo,
I'll show you the nettle-place
    On my leg,
If you'll lay me a great big
    Eastery egg."

The Little Black Hen
    Said, "I don't care
For a How-do-you-do
    Or a Big-brown-bear,
But I'll lay you a beautiful
    Eastery egg,
If you'll show me the nettle-place
    On your leg."

I showed her the place
    Where I had my sting.
She touched it gently
    With one black wing.
"Nettles don't hurt
    If you count to ten.
And now for the egg,"
    Said the Little Black Hen.

26

When I wake up
  On Easter Day,
I shall see my egg
  She's promised to lay.
If I were Emperors,
  If I were Kings,
It couldn't be fuller
  Of wonderful things.

Berryman and Baxter,
  Prettiboy and Penn,
And Old Farmer Middleton
  Are five big men.
All of them are wanting
  An egg for their tea,
But the Little Black Hen is much too busy,
The Little Black Hen is *much* too busy,
The Little Black Hen is MUCH too busy...
  She's laying my egg for me!

A. A. Milne

27

HAPPY BIRTHDAY AROUND THE WORLD

Did you know that...

...in Italy, every year on Carlotta's and Antonio's birthday, the twins get a pail of water dumped over their heads. Why? To help them grow, of course!

...in Denmark, Hans's mother serves a special pastry that looks like a giant pretzel. It's decorated with tiny flags. A big flag in the garden is raised, letting all the neighbors know it's Hans's birthday.

. . .in Thailand, Nid celebrates her birthday with a custom called "freeing the animals." She gets one small toy animal for each year—and one to grow on. Imagine receiving all those toy animals!

. . .in Hawaii, in the United States, Kalei finds his birthday gifts in a big bowl called a calabash by his front door. His family and friends celebrate with a luau complete with flower garlands, a roast pig, and festive music.

. . .in India, Sakti and her friends don't receive any gifts on their birthdays. Instead, they *give* gifts. They invite poor and orphaned children to their parties and shower them with presents and sweets.

29

T.J.'s Special Fourth of July

by Michael J. Pellowski

appy birthday to you," sang the children ringed around the picnic table in the Jones's backyard. The table and the yard were gaily decorated with lots of balloons and long streamers of many colors.

Little Thomas Jefferson Jones smiled as his friends continued to sing. Thomas Jefferson felt very proud of himself. He was proud to be named after a famous American patriot, even though everyone always called him T.J. for short. He was proud because today he was seven years old. But, most of all, he was proud because he was born on a very special day. T.J. Jones's birthday was on the Fourth of July, America's Independence Day. T.J.'s Uncle Samuel said being born on the Fourth of July made T.J. a real Yankee Doodle Dandy.

The Fourth of July was a great day to be born on. Earlier that morning, there had been a big parade on T.J.'s street. Bright red fire engines blasted their sirens, and high school bands marched along playing patriotic songs. And after the parade, six of T.J.'s friends were dropped off by their parents for T.J.'s birthday party.

"Happy birthday dear T.J., happy birthday to you," T.J.'s friends finished singing. T.J. grinned and took a deep breath. WHOOSH! He blew out the glowing candles on his cake and everyone clapped.

"What did you wish for?" T.J.'s mom asked as she started to cut the cake.

"I wished Uncle Sam could be here for my birthday," T.J. replied.

"Uncle Sam would like to be here, but he has to work," T.J.'s dad reminded him. "If he didn't work on Independence Day, there would be no fireworks display at night."

T.J. knew his father was right, but he missed Uncle Sam anyway. Uncle Sam was a fireworks expert. He was in charge of the town's annual Fourth of July fireworks show. People came from near and far to watch Uncle Sam's fabulous fireworks display.

31

"Cheer up," T.J.'s mom said as she put a piece of cake on his plate. "Uncle Sam can't be here, but you know he'd never forget your birthday."

T.J. perked up. Uncle Sam always gave him a terrific present. One time he gave T.J. a bright red wagon. Another time Uncle Sam brought him a remote control car. And last year, T.J.'s gift from his favorite uncle was an official baseball catcher's mitt.

"Where is Uncle Sam's present?" T.J. asked his dad.

"Uncle Sam told me he'd give you your present tonight when he's finished working," T.J.'s dad said. "He said it's a very special present for your very special seventh birthday."

T.J. smiled. Now he had two reasons to look forward to the end of the day. First, he would go to the fairgrounds to watch the fireworks show. Second, Uncle Sam would give him his birthday present.

When they finished eating cake and ice cream, T.J.'s friends watched him open his presents—a train set from the Baxter twins, a stuffed elephant from Peter, a board game from Shelly, a baseball cap from Amy, and a book about dinosaurs from David. "Now it's time to play party games!" announced T.J.'s dad. Everyone cheered. T.J. cheered the loudest. First they played blindman's buff. Next they played musical chairs. T.J. was the first player to lose a seat. But when they played pin the tail on the donkey, T.J. took first place.

"Did you have a nice day?" T.J.'s dad asked after the children had all gone home.

"Yes," said T.J. "But I can't wait until tonight." He smiled as he thought about the fireworks display and Uncle Sam's present.

Before long, it was time for the fireworks show. The Jones family drove to the county fairgrounds. The fairgrounds were decorated with American flags of all sizes and shapes. There were streamers and red, white, and blue balloons, too. Cheerful people were everywhere—playing softball, picnicking on the lawn, and gathering around the grandstand, where a band played festive music. T.J. felt happy.

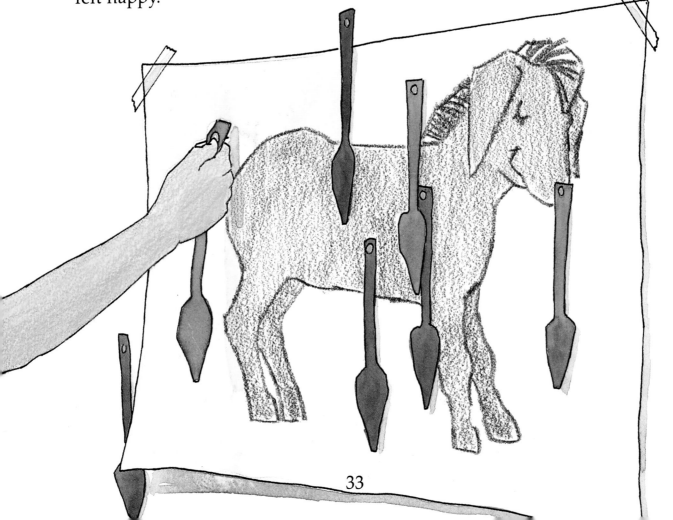

T.J. and his parents sat down near the grandstand. It was decorated with large American flags. When it was dark enough, the band stopped playing and the mayor walked up on the grandstand. "Welcome to our Fourth of July show," he said. "Now let the fireworks begin!" At that instant, a rocket shot high up into the dark sky. KA-BOOM! It exploded, sending twinkling embers shimmering toward the ground far below. BOOM! BOOM! BOOM! Rocket after rocket sailed skyward and exploded.

"Uncle Sam is doing a good job tonight," T.J. said as the explosions echoed above. KA-BOOM! KA-BLAM! KA-POW! One after another the fireworks exploded. The crowd watched in awe, marveling at the glorious sights and sounds of the Fourth of July celebration.

After the rockets had been whizzing skyward for quite some time, the mayor once again stood up. "Now it's time for the grand finale!" he announced as the crowd cheered.

"This should be good," T.J. said to his folks. "Uncle Sam always does something special to close the show."

Mr. Jones laughed. "I wonder what the finale will be?" he said. And seconds later. . .WHOOSH! The big fireworks board beyond the grandstand began to sparkle and glow. Suddenly, giant twinkling letters of red, white, and blue spelled out a very special message in the dark sky. T.J.'s eyes opened wide in surprise as the crowd clapped and cheered in delight. The message read: HAPPY FOURTH OF JULY BIRTHDAY TO T.J., A REAL YANKEE DOODLE DANDY!

Thomas Jefferson Jones began to clap, too. His Uncle Sam had made him very happy. "This is the best present of all!" said T.J. "I'll never ever forget my seventh birthday."

Hallowe'en

Hallowe'en's the time for nuts
        And for apples, too,
And for funny faces that
        Stare and glare at you.
Right behind them is a friend,
        Jack or Bob or Bess.
Isn't it the greatest fun
        When you try to guess?

Anna Medary

Bob

Bess

Jack

Jack, Bob, and Bess are getting ready to dress up in their
Halloween costumes.

36

Can you guess which is Jack?
Can you guess which is Bob?
Can you guess which is Bess?

Teeny Tiny Woman

A Traditional Halloween Tale

nce upon a time there was a teeny tiny woman who lived in a teeny tiny house.

One day this teeny tiny woman put on her teeny tiny bonnet and went out of her teeny tiny house to take a teeny tiny walk.

When she had gone a teeny tiny way, she came to a teeny tiny gate. The teeny tiny woman opened the teeny tiny gate and went into a teeny tiny churchyard.

In the teeny tiny churchyard the teeny tiny woman saw a teeny tiny bone, and she said to her teeny tiny self, "This teeny tiny bone will make me some teeny tiny soup for my teeny tiny supper."

So the teeny tiny woman put the teeny tiny bone into her teeny tiny basket and went home to her teeny tiny house.

When the teeny tiny woman got home to her teeny tiny house, she was a teeny tiny bit tired. She went up the teeny tiny stairs to her teeny tiny bed and put the teeny tiny bone into a teeny tiny cupboard.

When the teeny tiny woman had been asleep a teeny tiny time, she was awakened by a teeny tiny voice from the teeny tiny cupboard which said, "Give me my bone!"

The teeny tiny woman was a teeny tiny bit frightened, so she hid her teeny tiny head under the teeny tiny covers and went to sleep again.

And when she had been asleep a teeny tiny time, the teeny tiny voice cried out again from the teeny tiny cupboard a teeny tiny bit louder.

"Give me my bone!"

This made the teeny tiny woman a teeny tiny bit more frightened, so she hid her teeny tiny head a teeny tiny bit farther under the teeny tiny covers.

And when she had been asleep again for a teeny tiny time, the teeny tiny voice from the teeny tiny cupboard said again a teeny tiny bit louder, "GIVE ME MY BONE!"

The teeny tiny woman was a teeny tiny bit more frightened, but she popped her teeny tiny head out from the teeny tiny covers and said in her loudest teeny tiny voice,

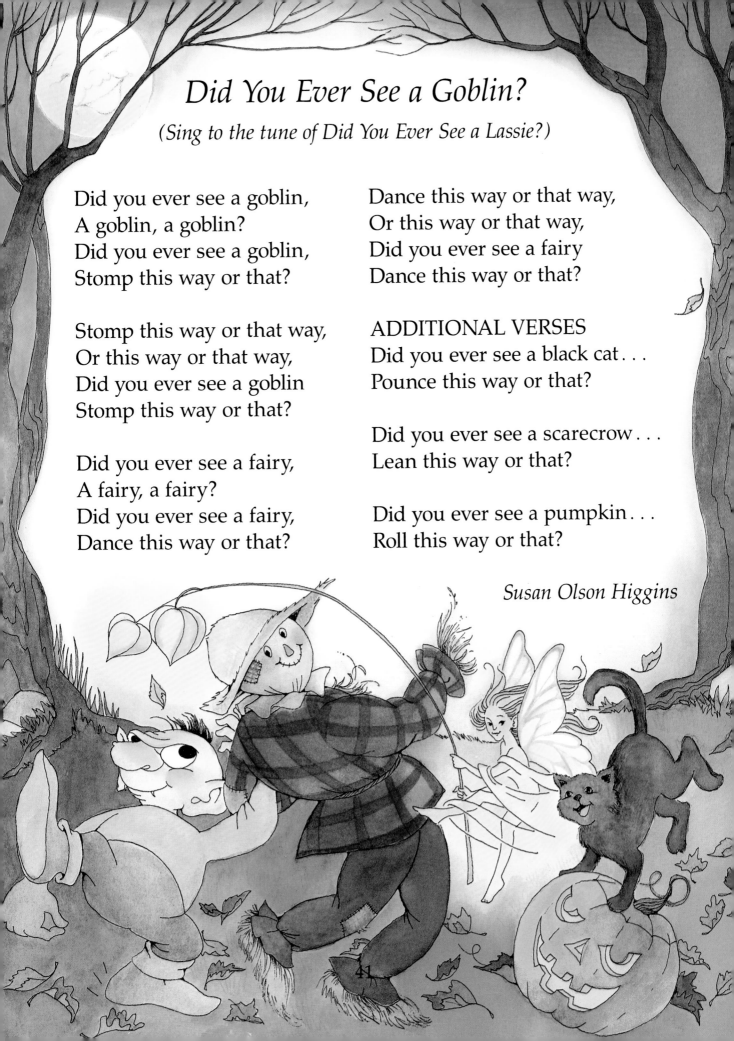

Did You Ever See a Goblin?

(Sing to the tune of Did You Ever See a Lassie?)

Did you ever see a goblin,
A goblin, a goblin?
Did you ever see a goblin,
Stomp this way or that?

Stomp this way or that way,
Or this way or that way,
Did you ever see a goblin
Stomp this way or that?

Did you ever see a fairy,
A fairy, a fairy?
Did you ever see a fairy,
Dance this way or that?

Dance this way or that way,
Or this way or that way,
Did you ever see a fairy
Dance this way or that?

ADDITIONAL VERSES
Did you ever see a black cat . . .
Pounce this way or that?

Did you ever see a scarecrow . . .
Lean this way or that?

Did you ever see a pumpkin . . .
Roll this way or that?

Susan Olson Higgins

The First Thanksgiving

by Wendy Wax

These are the Pilgrims.

These are the Indians.

Many years ago, over 100  from England sailed

on a  called the Mayflower across the Atlantic Ocean.

They wanted to find a new homeland where they could have their

freedom. The  was very crowded. Sometimes

the played, hiding on a small on the upper

deck. But, most of the journey was no fun at all. Stormy weather

brought rough  . Many  got sick and

some died.

Two months later, in early November, the  reached

Cape Cod Bay. A captain, named Miles Standish, and some other

 went ashore in a small fishing . They

searched for a place to settle. One day, they found the perfect

spot—it had rich soil, fresh , and

The settled into this new homeland, which they

called Plymouth Plantation.

The weren't prepared for the long, cold winter.

There was a lot of sickness and death. Only three families made it

through the winter!

When spring came, an from the Wampanoag tribe,

named Samoset, came to Plymouth. The  were afraid

of until he said, "Welcome, Englishmen!" in English.

Since only knew a few words of English, he brought

back an named Squanto, who knew English well.

 also brought Chief Massasoit, the leader of his tribe,

and other 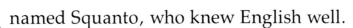, too. Chief Massasoit and Governor

Bradford had a meeting, and 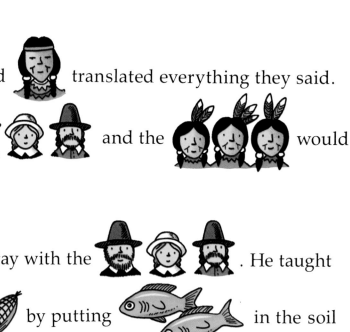 translated everything they said.

They decided that the 👒👒👒 and the 🪶🪶🪶 would

be friends.

🪶 decided to stay with the 👒👒👒. He taught

them how to plant 🌽🌽 by putting 🐟🐟 in the soil

to make the 🌽🌽 grow taller. 🪶 also taught

them to fish and hunt. The fall harvest was so good that

the 👒👒👒 planned to have a feast to thank their 🪶🪶🪶

friends. The 👒👒 went hunting and 🎣.

The 👒👒 picked 🌰🌰 and 🫐🫐, plucked 🐔🐔, and

baked 🍞. The 👧👦 helped with everything.

The 👒👒👒 were surprised when, on Thanksgiving Day,

almost 100 🪶🪶🪶 showed up! The 🪶🪶🪶 brought

five 🦌 so there would be enough food. Everyone sat

under the  —some at long 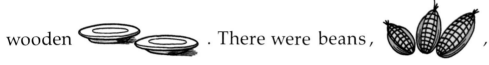 under

the and others on the .

There was a lot of food, which everyone ate off of

wooden . There were beans, ,

stewed pumpkins, squash, 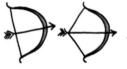, , ,

duck, and . And everything tasted delicious!

After the feast, the danced and showed

the  how they could shoot with .

Captain Standish led the  as they marched in a parade.

The played together. It was so much fun, that

the  stayed for three days!

That is the story of the first Thanksgiving. The land that the Pilgrims were thankful for then is now the United States of America. Today, American families celebrate Thanksgiving on the fourth Thursday of November. They are very thankful for the good things in life, and they remember the brave Pilgrims and friendly Indians who had the first Thanksgiving dinner long ago.

Turkeys Move in the Strangest Way

Turkeys move in the strangest way,
    Whenever they go to the forest to play.

Flying to the branches,
    they flutter, flutter, flutter,
(Flap your arms like a turkey.)

Walking to the meadow
    they strut, strut, strutter!
*(Strut stiff-legged with your chest out
and chin up.)*

Stepping over acorns,
    they wobble, wobble, wobble!

And they NEVER stop talking
    with a gobble, gobble, gobble!
(Rock back and forth from foot to foot.)
(Pull at the skin under your chin.)

When turkeys hurry
    to a hiding spot,
They scurry, scurry, scurry
    with a trot, trot, trot!
*(Run around in a circle,
lifting your knees high.)*
GOBBLE! GOBBLE!

Susan Olson Higgins

CELEBRATING CHANUKAH

Chanukah is an eight-day holiday observed in December by Jewish people all over the world. They observe it to remember their victory over the Syrians 2,000 years ago. Back then, the Jews had only enough oil to light their temple for a day. But, to their surprise, that tiny bit of oil burned for eight days.

David and Lori's family celebrates Chanukah. This year, Lori is old enough to help light the *menorah*, a special candle holder. It has places for eight candles — one for each night the oil burned — plus an extra candle, the *shammash*, which is used to light one candle on the first night, two on the second night, and so on. Every night of the holiday, one more candle is added.

The house is filled with good smells. David helps Grandma make potato pancakes called *latkes*. Lori likes hers topped with sour cream. But David's favorite is applesauce.

Each night of Chanukah, David and Lori get a small present. Tonight, Lori unwraps a book on Chanukah. David gets a small spinning top called a *dreidel*. But the best gift of all is Chanukah *gelt*, or candy money, from Grandma.

After dinner, David and Lori play with the dreidel. Each of them puts a coin into a pile called the *pot*. First, Lori spins the dreidel. Round and round it goes. Each of the dreidel's four sides has a Hebrew letter with a special meaning: *gimmel*, take the pot; *nun*, take nothing; *shin*, put one coin in; *hay*, take half the pot. It lands on *gimmel*, which means Lori wins the whole pot!

Later, Grandma reads from Lori's new book. "In Mexico and India," says Grandma, "people light tiny oil lamps instead of menorahs. And in some countries, fried doughnuts filled with jelly and rolled in powdered sugar are favorite Chanukah treats."

Malke's Secret Recipe

A Chanukah Story by David A. Adler

In Chelm, as in other towns, each family had its own latke recipe. In some families the recipe had been handed down from mother to daughter for many generations. Some people added just salt and pepper to the potatoes. Others added eggs and onions. There were even people who added paprika, parsley, and bread crumbs.

Most people were happy to share their latke recipes. But not Malke, the tailor's wife.

"I may be a poor woman," Malke said, "but I make the best latkes in Chelm, and I'm the only one who has the recipe."

When Malke was a young bride, she would let people taste her latkes. She wanted everyone to know how good they were. But Malke became afraid that someone eating her latkes might be able to taste each ingredient and learn her recipe. Since then, she only let her husband and children eat her famous latkes.

As the years passed, Malke's latkes tasted even better in people's memories than they had tasted on their forks.

Berel, the shoemaker, always closed his eyes and smiled when he remembered Malke's latkes. "They were so very soft," he would tell his wife Yentel, "and so very light. Eating Malke's latkes was like eating a cloud."

Then one Chanukah night, Berel, Yentel, and their children were eating latkes. These were not soft and light latkes, but thick, heavy ones.

Berel took one bite and banged on the table. "Enough!" he shouted. "I'm tired of the same latkes every Chanukah. Tomorrow I'm getting Malke's recipe."

The next morning Berel told Yentel, "I'm not opening the shop

today. If someone comes with his shoes, tell him to come back tomorrow. But don't tell him where I've gone."

Berel hid behind a tree near Malke's house. He waited there all day, but Malke didn't make latkes.

That night, Berel watched as Malke and her family lit their Chanukah candles. He heard them sing *Maoz Tzur,* "Rock of Ages," and he watched them play dreidel.

Then Berel saw Malke take out some potatoes, a grater, and a large pan.

"This is it!" Berel said to himself. "Tonight I will eat latkes as soft and light as a cloud."

Berel crawled close to the window. He watched and wrote down everything Malke did.

When the latkes were done, Berel ran home to his wife Yentel.

"I've got it!" he said. "I've got Malke's recipe."

Berel looked at his paper. "First take five potatoes and two eggs," he read.

"Some secret recipe," Yentel said as she watched Berel peel the potatoes. "We always use potatoes and eggs."

Berel grated the potatoes into a bowl. He added the eggs.

"We do that, too," Yentel said.

"Now," Berel read. "Chop six scallions very fine."

"Scallions!" Yentel said. "Who ever heard of using scallions in latkes? Everyone uses an onion. An onion is better."

"So I'll use an onion," Berel said. He chopped it and mixed it in with the potatoes.

"Next," Berel said, "Malke mixed in flour."

"Don't use flour. Use bread crumbs," Yentel said.

Berel used bread crumbs.

Berel added some salt. He looked down at his paper and was about to add pepper when Yentel shook her head and said, "Pepper makes me sneeze."

Berel didn't add the pepper.

"Now I need a lemon," Berel said. "Malke squeezed in a few drops of lemon juice."

Yentel shook her head. "No. Lemon juice belongs in tea."

"And Malke added parsley," Berel continued. "She made her latkes very thin and fried them in vegetable oil."

"Parsley! Vegetable oil! That's not a secret recipe. That's secret nonsense," Yentel said. "Parsley belongs in a salad with carrots. In

this house we fry in chicken fat. And thick latkes taste better than thin ones."

Berel and Yentel made their latkes with potatoes, eggs, salt, and bread crumbs, just like they always did. They made their latkes very thick and fried them in chicken fat.

When the latkes were done, Berel and Yentel and their children sat down to eat them. They ate slowly. They wanted to know if Malke's latkes really did taste better than anyone else's.

"These latkes don't taste soft and light," one of the children said.

"And they don't taste like clouds," another added.

"Some secret recipe," Berel told Yentel after all the latkes were eaten. "They taste just like ours."

"Well," Yentel said, "this just proves that no matter how you make them, latkes always taste the same."

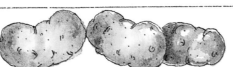

Merry Christmas

I saw on the snow
when I tried my skis
the track of a mouse
beside some trees.

Before he tunneled
to reach his house
he wrote "Merry Christmas"
in white, in mouse.

Aileen Fisher

This little mouse needs some help in
decorating his big Christmas tree.
The decorations are hidden in the woods.
Can you find them? How do you think
the mouse should decorate the tree?

CHRISTMAS CUSTOMS AROUND THE WORLD

There are so many things to love about Christmastime! What's your favorite?

In Mexico, Lupita is having a Christmas party. She and her friends take turns trying to break open the piñata—a bright decoration that's shaped like an animal. When it's Lupita's turn—WHACK!—she cracks the piñata open! Candies and toys spill out everywhere!

John knows Christmas has come to England—everyone's putting up decorations. John's mom ties a huge red bow to the wreath on their front door. His dad turns on the colored lights. "It looks great!" shouts John's friend Sandy.

In the United States, Lauren has hung up her stocking and gone to bed—but she's almost too excited to sleep! She listens for the sound of reindeer on the roof. Did Santa Claus get the letter she sent to the North Pole? Will he remember what she asked for?

Greta's favorite is the Christmas tree—a custom that began in her country of Germany. Her parents keep the tree hidden until Christmas Eve. At last Greta gets to unlock the door. "How beautiful!" she cries.

Sweets!—that's what Jean Pierre in France likes the best! He's learning how to make a bûche de Noël—a chocolate cake shaped like a Yule log. What a mess they make! "Ah, well," says Mama. "That's part of the fun!" While it's baking, Jean Pierre puts his shoes out on the hearth—for more treats that le père Noël, the French name for Santa Claus, will bring.

A Visit from St. Nicholas

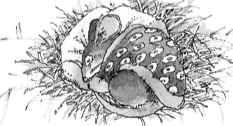

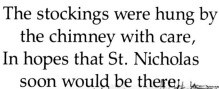

The stockings were hung by
the chimney with care,
In hopes that St. Nicholas
soon would be there;

'Twas the night before Christmas,
when all through the house
Not a creature was stirring,
not even a mouse;

The children were nestled all
snug in their beds,
While visions of sugarplums
danced in their heads;
And mamma in her kerchief,
and I in my cap,
Had just settled our brains for
a long winter's nap—

When out on the lawn there
arose such a clatter,
I sprang from my bed to see
what was the matter.
Away to the window I flew
like a flash,
Tore open the shutters and
threw up the sash.

The moon, on the breast of
the new-fallen snow,
Gave a luster of midday to
objects below;

When what to my wondering
eyes should appear
But a miniature sleigh and
eight tiny reindeer,

With a little old driver, so
lively and quick,
I knew in a moment it must
be St. Nick.
More rapid than eagles his
coursers they came,

And he whistled, and shouted,
and called them by name:
"Now, Dasher! now, Dancer!
now, Prancer and Vixen!
On, Comet! on, Cupid! on,
Donder and Blitzen!
To the top of the porch, to
the top of the wall!

Now, dash away, dash away,
dash away all!"
As dry leaves that before the
wild hurricane fly,
When they meet with an
obstacle, mount to the sky,
So up to the house-top the
coursers they flew,
With the sleigh full of toys—
and St. Nicholas too.

And then in a twinkling,
  I heard on the roof
The prancing and pawing of
  each little hoof.
As I drew in my head, and was
  turning around,
Down the chimney St. Nicholas
  came with a bound.
He was dressed all in fur from
  his head to his foot,
And his clothes were all
  tarnished with ashes and soot;

A bundle of toys he had flung
  on his back,
And he looked like a peddler
  just opening his pack.
His eyes how they twinkled!
  his dimples how merry!
His cheeks were like roses, his
  nose like a cherry;
His droll little mouth was
  drawn up like a bow,
And the beard on his chin was
  as white as the snow.

The stump of a pipe he held
  tight in his teeth,
And the smoke it encircled his
  head like a wreath.
He had a broad face and a
  little round belly
That shook, when he laughed,
  like a bowl full of jelly.
He was chubby and plump, a
  right jolly old elf,
And I laughed, when I saw
  him, in spite of myself.

A wink of his eye and a twist
   of his head
Soon gave me to know I had
   nothing to dread.
He spoke not a word, but
   went straight to his work,
And filled all the stockings;
   then turned with a jerk,

And laying his finger aside of
   his nose,
And giving a nod, up the
   chimney he rose.
He sprang to his sleigh, to his
   team gave a whistle,
And away they all flew like
   the down of a thistle;
But I heard him exclaim, ere
   he drove out of sight,

"Happy Christmas to all, and
   to all a good-night!"

Clement C. Moore

63

Little People™ Big Book About HOLIDAYS AND CELEBRATIONS

TIME-LIFE for CHILDREN™

Publisher: Robert H. Smith
Managing Editor: Neil Kagan
Editorial Directors: Jean Burke Crawford,
　　　　Patricia Daniels
Editorial Coordinator: Elizabeth Ward
Marketing Director: Ruth P. Stevens
Product Manager: Margaret Mooney
Production Manager: Prudence G. Harris
Administrative Assistant: Rebecca C. Christoffersen
Editorial Consultants: Jacqueline A. Bell, Sara Mark

PRODUCED BY PARACHUTE PRESS, INC.

Editorial Director: Joan Waricha
Editors: Christopher Medina, Jane Stine,
　　　　Wendy Wax
Writers: Cathy East Dubowski, Michael J.
　　　　Pellowski, H.L. Ross, Wendy Wax
Designer: Greg Wozney
Illustrators: Shirley Beckes (p. 16-17, 36-37, 46-47),
　　　　Joan Holub (p. 6-9, 28-29, 50-55), Anni
　　　　Matsick (p. 30-35), Pat Merrell (p. 42-
　　　　45), John Speirs (cover, p. 4-5, 18-23,
　　　　56-57, 60-63), John Wallner (p. 10-15,
　　　　38-40), Randi Wasserman (p. 24-27,
　　　　48-49, 58-59), Linda Weller (p. 41)

Time-Life Books Inc. is a wholly owned subsidiary of THE TIME INC. BOOK COMPANY.

TIME-LIFE is a trademark of Time Warner Inc. U.S.A.

FISHER-PRICE, LITTLE PEOPLE and AWNING DESIGN are trademarks of Fisher-Price, Division of The Quaker Oats Company, and are used under license.

Time-Life Books Inc. offers a wide range of fine publications, including home video products. For subscription information, call 1-800-621-7026, or write TIME-LIFE BOOKS, P.O. Box C-32068, Richmond, Virginia 23261-2068.

ACKNOWLEDGMENTS

Every effort has been made to trace the ownership of all copyrighted material and to secure the necessary permissions to reprint these selections. If any question arises as to the use of any material, the editor and the publisher, while expressing regret for any inadvertent error, will make the necessary correction in future printings.

Grateful acknowledgment is made to the following for permission to reprint copyrighted material: Doubleday (div. of Bantam, Doubleday, Dell Pub. Group, Inc.) for "New Year's Day" from A LITTLE BOOK OF DAYS by Rachel Field; and "Celebration" by Alonzo Lopez, from THE WHISPERING WIND by Terry Allen. Copyright © 1972 by Institute of American Indian Arts. E.P. Dutton (a div. of Penguin Books USA) for US rights for "Little Black Hen" from NOW WE ARE SIX by A.A. Milne. Copyright © 1927 by E.P. Dutton, renewed 1955 by A.A. Milne. Aileen Fisher for British Commonwealth rights to "Merry Christmas" from FEATHERED ONES AND FURRY by Aileen Fisher. Copyright © 1971 by Aileen Fisher. Harper & Row Publishers Inc. for US and Canadian rights for "Merry Christmas" from FEATHERED ONES AND FURRY by Aileen Fisher (Thomas Y. Crowell). Copyright © 1971 by Aileen Fisher. Susan Olson Higgins for "Turkeys Move In The Strangest Way" from THE THANKSGIVING BOOK, and "Did You Ever See A Goblin?" from THE HALLOWEEN BOOK by Susan Olson Higgins. Kar-Ben Copies, Inc. for MALKE'S SECRET RECIPE, A CHANUKAH STORY by David Adler. McClelland and Stewart Ltd. for Canadian rights to "Little Black Hen" from NOW WE ARE SIX by A.A. Milne. Mathuen Children's Books for British Commonwealth rights to "Little Black Hen" from NOW WE ARE SIX by A.A. Milne. Rand McNally for "Hallowe'en" by Anna Medary from Child Life Magazine. Copyright © 1926, 1954 by Rand McNally & Co. Yoshiko Uchida for "New Year's Hats for the Statues" from THE SEA OF GOLD AND OTHER TALES by Yoshiko Uchida. Copyright © 1965 by Yoshiko Uchida.

Library of Congress Cataloging-in-Publication Data

Little people big book about holidays and celebrations.
　　p. cm.
　　Summary: A collection of original stories, retellings, informational articles, poems, activities, and games about holidays.　ISBN 0-8094-7508-1.　ISBN 0-8094-7509-X (lib. bdg.)
　　1. Holidays—Literary collections. [1. Holidays—Literary collections.] I. Time-Life for Children (Firm)
PZ5.L725746 1990　　　　　　　　　　　　　　　　　　　　　　90-11037
810.8'033—dc20　　　　　　　　　　　　　　　　　　　　　　　　　CIP
　　　　　　　　　　　　　　　　　　　　　　　　　　　　　　　　AC

TIME-LIFE BOOKS
ALEXANDRIA, VIRGINIA

Celebration

I shall dance tonight.
When the dusk comes crawling,
There will be dancing
   and feasting.
I shall dance with the others
   in circles,
     in leaps,
      in stomps.
Laughter and talk
   will weave into the night,
Among the fires
   of my people.
Games will be played
And I shall be
   a part of it.

Alonzo Lopez